Happy Holidays

by Chaplain Peggi Trusty

A Greeting Card for the Holiday Season

From the Clear Water Card Collection

A Subsidiary of Whole Heart Media

www.ClearWaterCardCollection.com

CLEAR WATER
card collection

Happy Holidays
A Greeting Card for the Holiday Season

ISBN: 9781706072973
Imprint: Independently published

Copyright © 2019

All rights are reserved. No part of this publication may be reproduced, stored in a retrieval system or transmitted in any form or by any means, electronic, mechanical, photocopying, recording or otherwise, without prior permission of the author.

For more information about the author, please go to PeggiTrusty.com

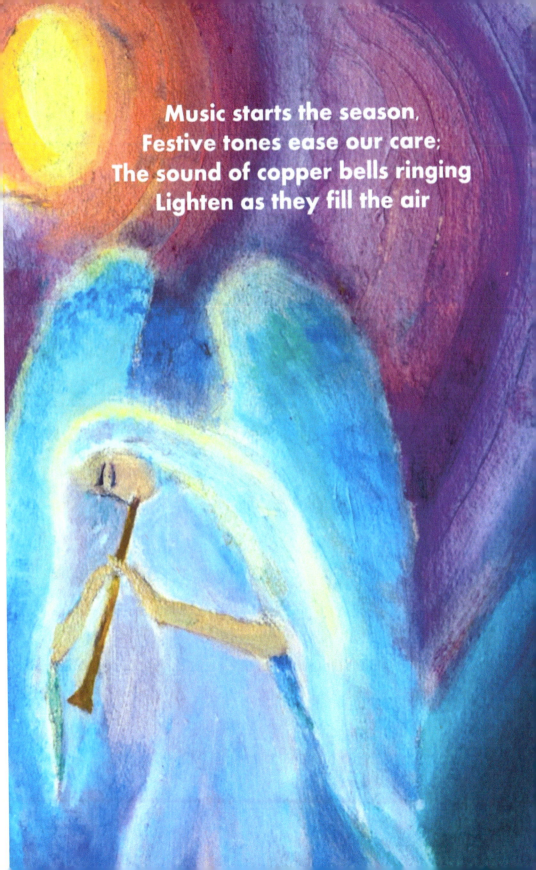

Music starts the season,
Festive tones ease our care;
The sound of copper bells ringing
Lighten as they fill the air

**Celebrations that follow close behind,
Have children bursting with delight.
So much laughter, so many smiles,
Days are full of sweetness and light**

A thousand thoughts
flood our minds,
From many winters
long ago.
Stories and games
and fairytales
Blanket our days
like new snow.

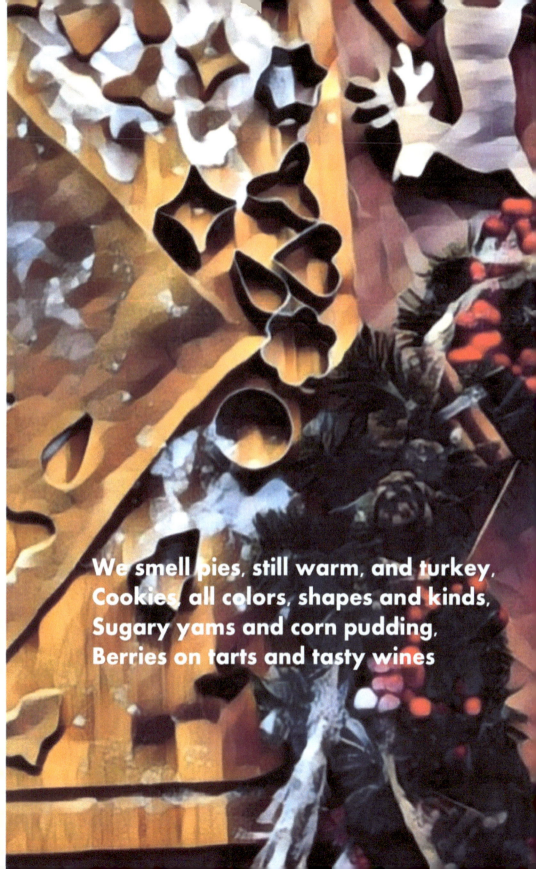

We smell pies, still warm, and turkey,
Cookies, all colors, shapes and kinds,
Sugary yams and corn pudding,
Berries on tarts and tasty wines

We buy perfect gifts
to wrap and hide,
Making sure that
no one is missed;
Then light candles
and pour sweet drinks,
Kindle fires
to snuggle and kiss

Beneath the razzle and dazzle,
Beyond the sparkles and the noise,
There is a quiet sort of peace,
The heart is ready to enjoy

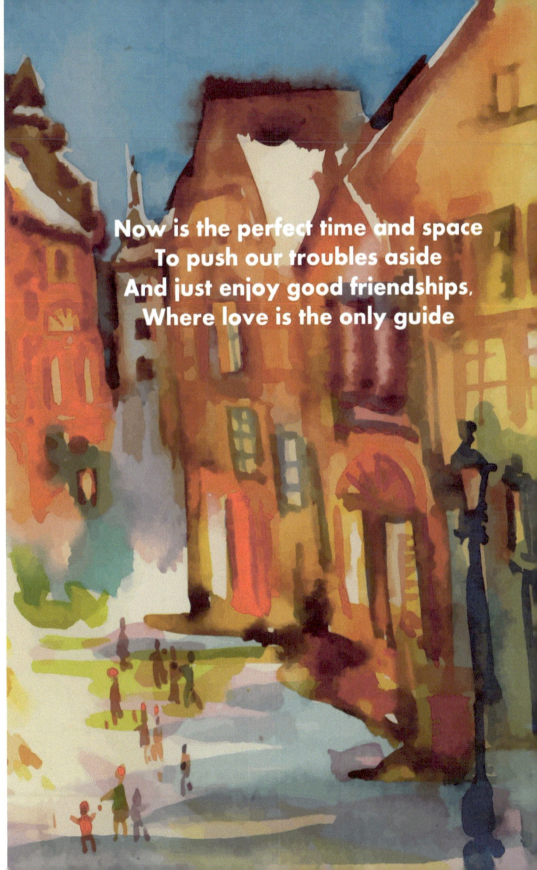

Now is the perfect time and space
To push our troubles aside
And just enjoy good friendships,
Where love is the only guide

Our joys,
not without sorrow,
Missing loved ones who've
passed from view,
Wrapping ourselves
in recollections,
Let the memories
smile back at you

Tis the season
to make new smiles,
With the passed and
present sprinkled in;
Add a dash of kindness
to gift a blessing
And the warmth of love
swells within

It's the time of year
when your wanting
Everyday
to be like this.
Hot cocoa in
your coffee cup;
A very special
kind of bliss

Imagine yourself a blessing,
Not just celebrating a day.
Become love, joy, kindness and peace,
Be the holiday on display

It's time to pause and consider
As we raise our glass in cheer.
Let us resolve to be better,
A blessing for the brand-new year

Printed in the USA
CPSIA information can be obtained
at www.ICGtesting.com
LVHW060844261024
794881LV00006B/25